FOCUS on FOOTBALL

CONTENTS

	page
The history	2
The most extraordinary game ever played!	4
Tips for strikers	6
Tips for defenders	8
Tips for goalkeepers	10
The referee - a difficult job!	12
Cups and competitions	14
Football stadiums of the world	16
Football and money	18
Football in Egypt	20
Egyptian stars abroad	22
The World Cup - 1990 and 1994	24
World football stars	26
The future of football	28
Quiz	30

Jeremy Taylor

Bill Shankly, who was the manager of Liverpool football club, said, "Some people say football is a matter of life and death. In fact, it's much more important than that!" But when and where did football begin?

The ancient Romans played a kind of football called "harpastum". There were few rules and many people got hurt.

In medieval Europe, football was a very dangerous game. The kings of France and England tried to stop it.

Did you know?
Italy played a game called "calcio" in the 16th century. It was like football, but there were 27 players on each side!

THE H

The Italians still call football "calcio" today.

The North American Indians played a game called "pasuckquakkohowog"! In this game they kicked a small ball around a field.

It was a strange kind of game. The two goals were more than a kilometre apart and there were about 1,000 players on each side!

In Central America, the Aztec Indians also played football hundreds of years ago. The team that lost a game were killed!

Some schools in England used to play football in the 19th century, but they often had different rules! So in 1846 the rules of football were written at the University of Cambridge.

In 1904 the International Football Federation (FIFA) was started. This organisation controls all international football. Egypt became a member of FIFA in 1921.

FIFA has more than 150 members. Almost every country in the world is a member.

THE MOST EX... GAME EV...

Between 1914 and 1918 many people in Europe were fighting in a war. Millions of men died in this war.

However, in the middle of one of the battles there was a football match! It happened near Ypres, France, on Christmas Day (25 December) 1914.

The German soldiers were fighting against the British soldiers. There was a piece of land between the two armies. It was called "no-man's-land".

On Christmas Day the two armies stopped fighting. The air was quiet for the first time in months. Then someone suggested a game of football.

...AORDINARY ... PLAYED!

At first the two armies did not trust each other. But slowly the soldiers came together. They shook hands and chose the best players. Then the match began.

It was an exciting game and after 90 minutes the Germans won the game. After the match the players left no-man's-land.

The next day, the men started fighting again. Many of the football players died.

page 5

One of the most important qualities of a good striker is speed. You must be able to run quickly.

It is not enough to shoot well - if you cannot run quickly you will not get the ball.

TIPS STRI

Did you know?
Saleh Selim scored 8 goals for El-Ahli in a match against El-Ismaili in 1958.

Amazing fact!
Stephen Stanis scored 16 goals in a match for Lens, France on 13 December 1942.

Good footballers practise running every day. Some teams train by running up and down sand dunes. This is very difficult, but it is good for leg muscles.

FOR KERS

Hossam Hassan, one of Egypt's top strikers

Good strikers must not only be quick; they must also be intelligent.

When you are playing, do not wait for the ball to come to you. You must move around. Try to get into a good position to receive a pass. A good striker will keep running for almost all the 90 minutes of a game.

Do you kick the ball with your left foot or your right? You can probably kick with only one of them.

But imagine you are playing in an important match. The ball comes to you and you must score a goal. The ball is on your "wrong" foot. Your team will not be happy if you can only score with one foot.

Practise shooting with your "bad" foot. It will take time but it is worth the practice.

What does a striker need to score a goal? He needs the ball and he needs space.

Your job as a defender is to stop him getting either of these.

Close marking stops the strikers from scoring

Each defender should "mark" one striker - this means you should stay near him all the time. Do not let him get into a space.

If you stay close to the striker, his team will find it difficult to pass to him. If they do not pass to him, he cannot score a goal!

page 8

FOR'DERS

A good striker can shoot at goal with his left or right foot. Many strikers prefer to use one of their feet only.

It will not take you long to find out which foot a striker likes to use. So how can you use this knowledge to help you as a defender?

In the picture above, the striker must shoot with his left foot.

Imagine that a striker is coming towards you with the ball. He must go past you to shoot at goal. If he is right-footed, stand a little to the left. This means it is not easy for him to shoot with his right foot.

A good striker can score a goal which could win a game. A good defender can stop a goal which could lose a game. They are equally important.

There was a match in Germany between Bayern Munich and Eintracht Frankfurt. The Bayern striker, Klaus Augenthaler, noticed that Eintracht's goalkeeper was a long way in front of his goal.

Augenthaler was only two metres inside the half-way line. But he tried a shot. He kicked the ball very hard and high.

The goalkeeper saw the ball coming. He also saw where it was going! He ran back very quickly, but he wasn't fast enough. Augenthaler scored an amazing goal!

Augenthaler's goal can be a good lesson for you. If you are a goalkeeper, make sure you are always in the right place.

FOR KEEPERS

Sometimes a striker has the ball and there is only the goalkeeper between him and the goal. What should the goalkeeper do?

A good goalkeeper will run out towards the striker. Why? Look at the two diagrams below.

In the first example the goalkeeper is staying on his line. The striker can see a lot of the goal.

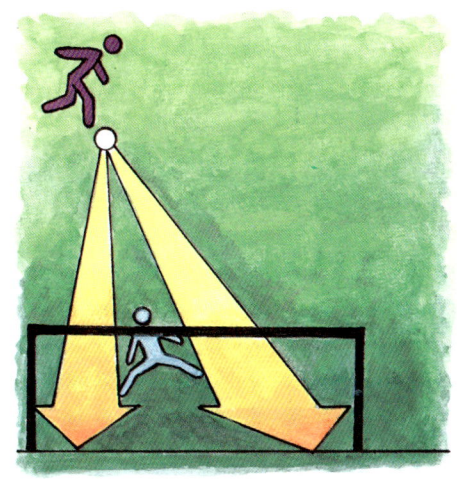

In the second example the goalkeeper is coming out towards the striker. In this way he reduces the area which the striker can see.

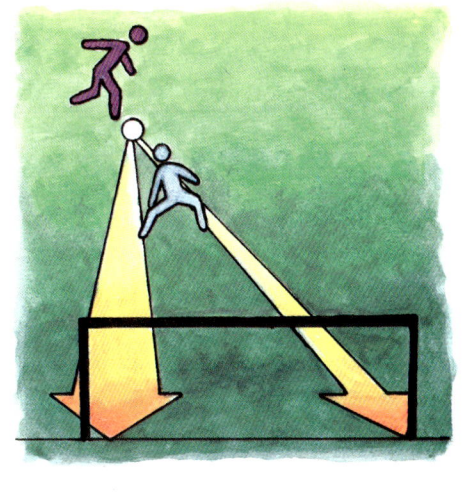

Next time you watch a match, look at how quickly the goalkeeper comes out of his goal.

During a match in England the goalkeeper came out of his goal to stop a striker. The striker shot over the goalkeeper's head.

The ball was going into the goal, but there was a defender standing on the line. The ball was high. The defender jumped into the air and punched the ball over the crossbar with his hand.

Everyone shouted for a penalty. But the referee gave a corner!

The next day a newspaper published a photograph. It showed the defender punching the ball. The referee said the sun had been in his eyes.

THE REFEREE — A DIFFICULT

Most referees hate television. With television you can watch something again and again. Was it a penalty? You can watch it again in "slow motion". Then you can decide. But a referee must decide immediately.

There may be 50,000 people in the stadium, and half of them are shouting "Penalty!" It is difficult to say no!

EREE
ULT JOB!

If a referee is not sure about something he may ask one of the two linesmen. There is one linesman for each half of the field.

Every referee must carry these things with him during a game:
- two watches,
- two whistles,
- two pens,
- a coin,
- a notebook,
- two cards -
  one yellow and one red

The red card is for sending players off. The yellow card is for warning them.

Amazing fact!
During a game in Peru, one of the players was not happy with the referee's decision. He left the field and came back with a gun. Then he shot the referee!

page 13

CUPS
COMPE

T he Frenchman Jules Rimet was the president of FIFA from 1921 until 1954. He helped to start the World Cup competition in 1930. The cup for the winners was called the Jules Rimet Cup.

Pelé with the World Cup in 1970

The Jules Rimet Cup was used until 1970 when Brazil won it for the third time. They beat Italy in the final. So they were allowed to keep this cup.

Did you know?
The first Women's World Cup was held in China in 1991. It was won by the women from the USA!

The Jules Rimet Cup disappeared in 1966 after England won it. It was stolen in London. A few days later a dog called Pickles was walking in a park in London with his master. What did he find under a tree? The missing World Cup!

Did you know?
The Egypt Cup started in 1921.

European countries play in the European Championship every four years. In 1992 the finals are in Sweden.

The most important competition for African national teams is the African Cup of Nations.

This competition started in 1957. Egypt won the first cup. They beat Sudan in the final in Alexandria. Egypt won again in 1959 and 1986.

Football became a part of the Olympic Games in 1900. Only amateur teams take part.

Egypt took fourth place in the Olympic Games of 1928 and 1964.

In the early games of football, people stood around the field to watch. But more and more people wanted to watch, so football clubs had to build stadiums.

Large modern stadiums cost millions of dollars to build. They sometimes include sports centres, social clubs and even shopping centres!

FOOTBALL OF THE

pitch

Did you know?
The oldest stadium in Egypt is the Alexandria stadium. It was built in 1928.

The biggest stadium in the world is the Maracaña stadium in Rio de Janeiro in Brazil. In 1950, more than 199,000 sat in it to watch the World Cup final between Brazil and Uruguay!

In the Da Luz stadium in Portugal, 127,000 people watched the final of the World Youth Championships in 1991. As in most modern stadiums, all the people in the Da Luz stadium have seats.

STADIUMS WORLD

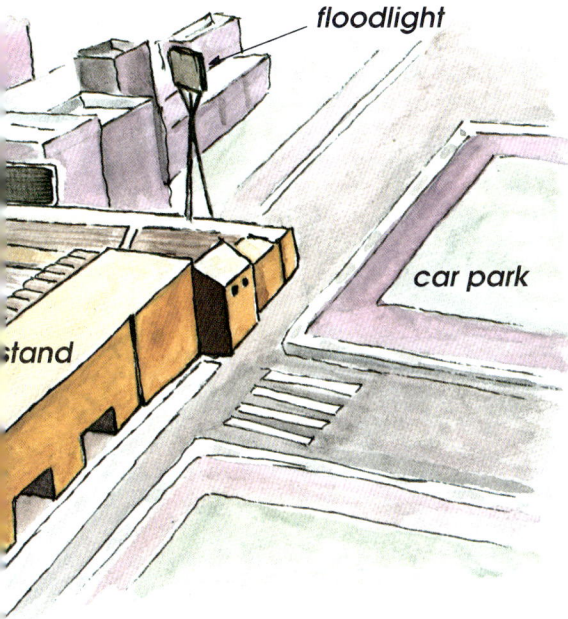

The biggest stadium in Egypt is the Cairo International stadium. It can hold 100,000 people.

However, in 1970 there was a famous African Cup Final in the stadium. It was between El-Ismaili and T. P. Inglebert from Zaire.

People started to arrive at the stadium in the early morning. When the match started, there were 130,000 people inside the stadium - and another 50,000 outside!

Cairo International Stadium, Nasr City

Do you know the name of El-Ahli club's stadium? It's the "Mokhtar el-Titch" Stadium.

Mokhtar el-Titch was one of El-Ahli's star defenders in the 1920s.

He got his name from the English. They called him "titch" - it means "small" in English!

page 17

Most football players in the world are amateurs. This means they do not get any money when they play a game.

Players who play football as a job are called professionals. Players in Egypt are amateurs.

Until the 1960s most footballers in Europe did not get much money. But then they wanted more money. Today many players earn thousands of dollars every month.

Football is big business. It costs a lot of money to run a football club. So where does the money come from?

Many companies give money to big football clubs. The players wear shirts with the name of a company on them. This is called sponsoring. The company sponsors the club. You can sometimes see this on the shirts of clubs in Egypt, too. National teams never wear sponsors' names.

There are also advertisements at the sides of the football field.

Big companies pay a lot of money for this, especially if the match is going to be on television.

In the 1980s, Egyptian television said it would not show football matches where there were advertisements around the field. This was because the television did not receive any of the money for the advertisements. But now you can see plenty of matches on television - and you can see the advertisements, too!

Did you know?
When Kuwait succeeded in going to the World Cup in Spain in 1982, the Crown Prince Sheikh Saad Abdallah Al Sabah gave many things to the 24 players. Each of them received a Cadillac, a new villa, some land, a gold watch and a speedboat!

Modern football started in Egypt in 1882. The British soldiers used to play against the Egyptians. Boys started to play in any spaces they could find. Later the square in front of the Citadel in Cairo was a famous place for matches!

El-Ahli and El-Zamalek are the most famous clubs in Egypt. But the oldest clubs are El-Sikka el-Hadeed and Olympi. They both started in 1905.

El-Ahli started playing football in 1907 and El-Zamalek in 1910.

Some of the clubs had foreign players. El-Zamalek were called El-Mokhtalat because the team was a mixture of Egyptian and foreign players. El-Zamalek became 100 per cent Egyptian in 1921.

The Egyptian Cup began in 1921. It is a "knock-out" competition - if a club loses a game it is "knocked out", it leaves the competition. The first winner was El-Zamalek.

Question What was El-Zamalek Club called before it became El-Mokhtalat? Answer Qasr el-Nil Club

The League started in 1948. El-Ahli won the competition nearly every year in the early years! Today there are four divisions in the league.

Many people think that Mahmoud El-Khateeb was one of the best players tEgypt has ever had. He is famous both for his football skills and for his good character. He played hard but fair.

El-Khateeb retired in 1989.

page 21

EGYPT STARS A

Have you heard of Hussain Higazy? He was the first man from Egypt to play football in another country.

He went to England in 1910 with his uncle. He studied at London University.

While he was at university he played football. He was a good player. Cambridge University heard about him and they asked him to come to them! So he went to Cambridge and won the top prize for football. After that he played for Fulham football club in London. He became very famous. Some people called him the "King of Football"! Hussain Higazy came back to Egypt in 1914.

After the World Cup in 1990 many football clubs in Europe and the Gulf came to Egypt to look at the top players. Sometimes they bought a player.

Ahmed Shubayr, the goalkeeper for El-Ahli, played well in the World Cup in Italy. Only two goals were scored against him. The English club Everton and the Scottish club Hibernian wanted to buy Shubayr, but he stayed at El-Ahli.

Ahmed Shubayr

page 22

EGYPTIAN ABROAD

In 1990 the Swiss club Neuchâtel bought two players, the twins Hossam and Ibrahim Hassan. Hany Ramsy also played for Neuchatel. This meant the Swiss team was more than 25% Egyptian!

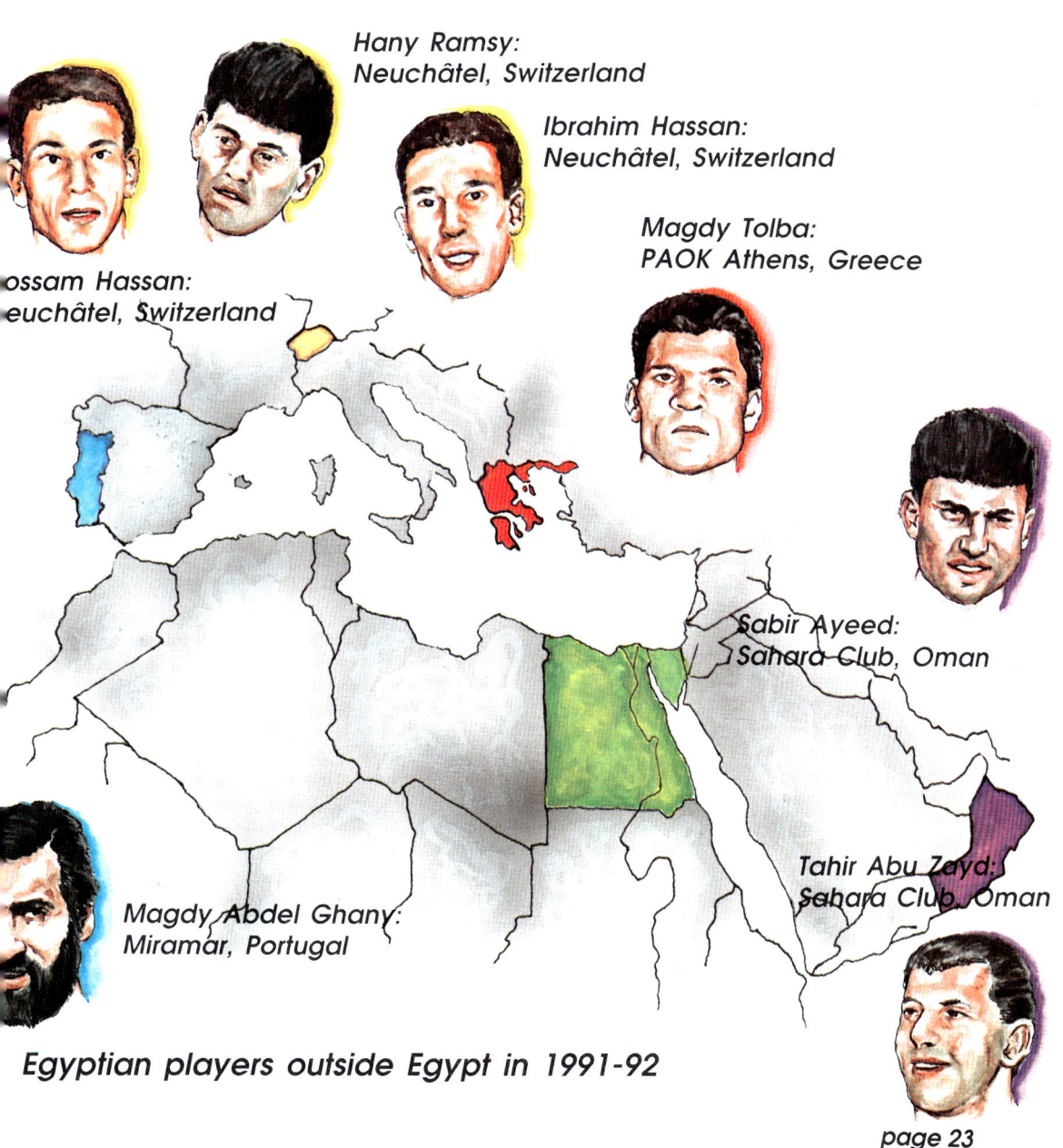

Hany Ramsy: Neuchâtel, Switzerland

Ibrahim Hassan: Neuchâtel, Switzerland

Magdy Tolba: PAOK Athens, Greece

Hossam Hassan: Neuchâtel, Switzerland

Sabir Ayeed: Sahara Club, Oman

Tahir Abu Zayd: Sahara Club, Oman

Magdy Abdel Ghany: Miramar, Portugal

Egyptian players outside Egypt in 1991-92

page 23

The 1990 World Cup was played in Italy. It was won by West Germany. But many people in Europe and South America now remember the football skills of the teams from Africa. It was only Egypt's second time in the World Cup finals. The first time was in 1934.

Egypt were in a difficult group with Holland (who won the European Championship in 1988), England and Ireland.

In an exciting match with Holland they had many chances to win, but the game ended in a draw. Egypt also drew with Ireland.

In Egypt's third game, England scored a goal in the last minutes of their game and "knocked out" Egypt.

The 1994 World Cup will be played in the USA. Football, or "soccer" as the Americans call it, is not yet very popular in the USA. Most Americans prefer to watch their own kind of football, called American Football.

Soccer clubs in the USA hope that more people in their country will want to play *their* game after 1994.

Amazing fact!
500,000,000 people in the world watched the 1990 World Cup final on television.

Who will win in 1994? Germany again? Brazil? Argentina? Or will there be a new name on the cup?

Cameroon also played very well in Italy. Their "secret weapon" was Roger Milla. At 39 years old, Milla had already stopped playing football. But he came back to play in the World Cup and helped Cameroon to reach the quarter-finals of the competition.

Roger Milla

Football is the most popular sport in the world. How many of these foreign stars do you know?

WORLD
ST

Gary Lineker (born 1960)
He played for Everton, Barcelona and Tottenham Hotspur and is the captain of England. In 1992 he went to the Japanese club Grampus Eight.

Lineker is a very fast striker. He scored six goals in the World Cup in 1986 - this was more than any other player. He has never been booked or sent off. He is a real gentleman!

Rud Guillet (born 1962)
He was born in Amsterdam, Holland, although his mother is from Surinam. He is famous for his football and his hair! He plays with his friend Marc van Basten, for AC Milan and Holland. AC Milan paid 11 million dollars to the Dutch club Eindhoven for him. He is the captain of Holland.

page 26

Lothar Matteus (born 1961)
He is a German striker who plays for Internazionale in Italy. The Italian club paid 3.5 million dollars to Bayern Munich for him! He was West Germany's captain when they won the 1990 World Cup.

But perhaps the most famous football player in the world is Edson Arantés do Nascimento. Do you know him? His other name is Pele! He played for Santos in Brazil. At the end of his football life he also played for the New York Cosmos. He played in three World Cup finals for Brazil - in 1958, 1962 and 1970. He scored more than 1,200 goals in his career! He played his last match in 1977.

In 1846 some men at Cambridge University wrote the rules of football. Since that time other people have changed some of the rules. Football is now more exciting and safer.

For example, strikers used to run into the goalkeeper while he was holding the ball. Today this is against the rules.

THE FUTURE OF FOOTBALL

FIFA controls the rules of football now. Some people would like to change these rules again. Here are two of the ideas they are thinking about:

1. Goalkeepers may not hold the ball for more than six seconds. Some goalkeepers today waste time by holding the ball when their team is winning.

2. FIFA may also change the offside rule. Many players do not like this rule. Also, it is often very difficult for the referee or linesman to see if a player is offside.

In 1992 FIFA made a new rule to stop players passing the ball back to the goalkeeper. This change will make football much more exciting.

What do you think of the ideas on page 28?

Here are some more ideas that FIFA may think about:
- They could make the goal wider so that strikers can score more goals.
- They could allow more substitutes, as in basketball and volleyball matches.

Football matches could be very different in future!

Why not send your own ideas to FIFA? See page 32 for their address.

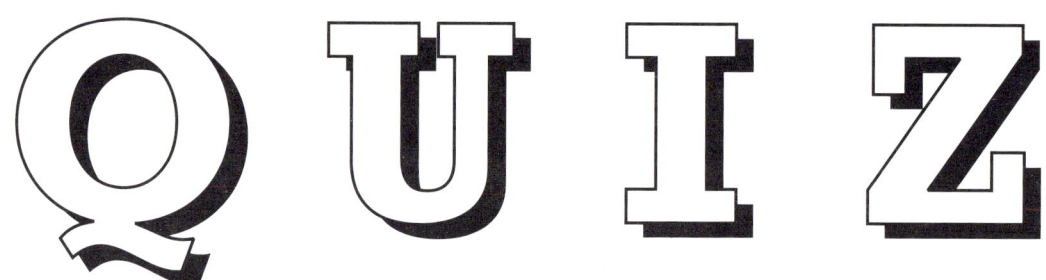

How much can you remember about "Focus on football"?

1. When was FIFA started?
   a 1314   b 1904   c 1921

2. When were the rules of football written?
   a 1846   b 1904   c 1921

3. When was the most extraordinary game of football ever played?
   a 25 December 1914   b 25 December 1918
   c 14 December 1925

4. The most important quality of a good goalkeeper is ...
   a to have big hands
   b to position himself well
   c to be very tall

5. Who won the World Cup for the third time in 1970?
   a England   b West Germany   c Brazil

6. Which is the biggest football stadium in the world?
   a Maracaña in Brazil   b Da Luz in Portugal
   c Wembley in England

7. How many people watched the World Cup final in 1950?
   a 19,000   b 1,900   c 199,000

page 30

8   What colour are the two cards that a referee carries?
    a red and blue   b yellow and blue   c red and yellow

9   When did the Egyptian football league start?
    a 1948   b 1938   c 1958

10 Which team did Roger Milla play for?
    a Brazil   b Cameroon   c Portugal

11 The 1994 World Cup will be played in ...
    a England   b Sweden   c the USA

12 Who was the captain of the team that won the World Cup in 1990?
    a Gary Lineker   b Rud Guillet   c Lothar Mattheus

ACTIVITY

Write the names of the teams in the football league this year, draw their uniforms and colour them.

EGYPTIAN LEAGUE AND CUP WINNERS 1981-1992		
	League	*Cup*
1981-82	El-Ahli	El-Ahli
1982-83	Arab Contractors	El-Ahli
1983-84	El-Zamalek	El-Ahli
1984-85	El-Ahli	El-Ahli
1985-86	El-Ahli	El-Tersana
1986-87	El-Ahli	*No competition*
1987-88	El-Zamalek	El-Zamalek
1988-89	El-Ahli	El-Ahli
1989-90	*No competition*	Arab Contractors
1990-91	El-Ismaili	El-Ahli
1991-92	El-Zamalek	El-Ahli

This book was first published jointly in 1992 by:

Elias Modern Publishing House
1 Keniset El Rum El Kathulik St.
Zaher, Cairo.Egypt.
PO Box 954 Cairo

and

Hoopoe Books
13 Rashdan St.
Missaha Square
Dokki, Cairo

Deposit no.1992/2925

© Elias-Hoopoe 1992

All rights reserved. No part of this book may be reproduced - mechanically, electronically or by any means, including photocopying - without written permission of the publishers

Illustrations and cover by
Joseph Hakeem

Printed by
Elias Modern Press,
Cairo

✉ **Address of FIFA** ✉

FIFA,
P.O. Box 85,
8030 Zurich,
Switzerland